Carter Cares

Marquita Battle

DEDICATION

This book is dedicated to my parents Malcolm and Mary Battle. Thank you for the beautiful life you have given my brother and me. Most importantly, thank you for teaching us to have LOVE in our hearts. I love you both dearly!

Carter was looking forward to seeing April at school. They were best friends in class and rode the bus home together. Carter waited and waited for her to get to class but she didn't show up. He asked Mrs. Lewis if she knew where April was and she told him she had the flu like he did last week.

Carter thought about April on the bus ride home. He missed her and was sad she was sick. Carter thought he somehow gave her the flu since he had just gotten over it and returned to school.

He cheered up once he thought about finally getting a new video game he had been saving his own money to buy.

Carter ran from the bus, entered his house, and to the kitchen for a drink of water.

Carter's mom always greeted him with a smile and a snack after school. His mom was not in the kitchen smiling as usual. Carter thought it was odd. He started to yell for his mom through the house until she answered. He didn't hear her until he was closer to his parent's room.

His mom was in the bed with cover and she was coughing. Carter thought his mom looked like he did when he had the flu the week before.

Carter's mom had the flu just like Carter and April. Oh no! He felt like it was his fault that his mom was sick since she took care of him while he was sick.

Carter knew he wanted to do something to help his mom and show that he cares.

Carter heard his dad walk in the door
from work.

He told his dad his ideas of tucking his mom in with blankets like she did for him, placing a hot towel on her forehead, or watching movies with her until she feels better.

Carter thought the best idea was to buy something that would make his mom feel better. He grabbed his piggy bank where all of the money was that he had been saving for the new video game.

Carter asked his dad to take him to the store to buy something to make his mom feel better.

Carter remembered what his mom gave him to get better. So he was looking for the same things. He grabbed apples, oranges, and bananas to keep her healthy.

Carter also picked up orange juice,
chicken noodle soup, and a box of saltine
crackers to help with her stomach ache
like he had with the flu.

Carter pretended he was a basketball player and shot a box into the basket.

His dad helped him to get the right medicine for the flu. The shopping was complete and it was time to pay for everything.

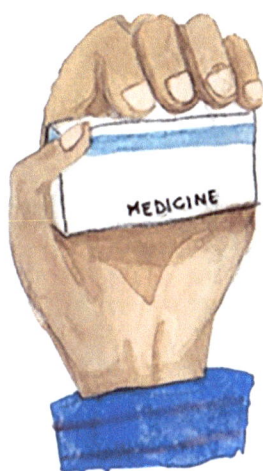

Carter walked to the counter at the store. His dad was close by but let him ring up the items all by himself.

The cashier finished scanning the items from Carter's basket. She asked him if he wasn't feeling well. Carter told her that his mom was sick so he was taking care of her like she took care of him when he was sick.

The cashier was happy and excited to hear about Carter's act of caring. She finished ringing everything up with a big smile on her face. The total was $22.36. His dad overheard the total. So he reached into his wallet to take out a credit card to pay for everything. Carter stopped him and told him that he wanted to pay with his own money.

His dad wanted to know how Carter had money to pay for all of the items. Carter explained that he took the money he was saving for the video game from his piggy bank to pay for the items. He wanted to take care of his mom like she took care of him. Carter's dad was so proud of his son for caring and allowed him to pay for the items.

Carter and his dad arrived home from the grocery store. His dad expressed how proud and full of joy he was with Carter's act of caring. He wanted to reward him by giving him enough money for three new video games.

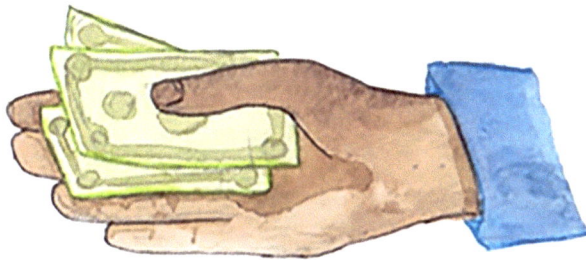

Carter was so happy that he couldn't stop smiling and hugging his dad.

www.ingramcontent.com/pod-product-compliance
Lightning Source LLC
LaVergne TN
LVHW072102070426
835508LV00002B/224